Creative Disobedience

Creative Disobedience

Dorothee Sölle
Translated by Lawrence W. Denef

Wipf & Stock
PUBLISHERS
Eugene, Oregon

Originally published in German as
Phantasie und Gehorsam: Überlegungen zu einer
künftigen christlichen Ethik.
© 1968 by Kreuz Verlag, Stuttgart.

Wipf and Stock Publishers
199 W 8th Ave, Suite 3
Eugene, OR 97401

Creative Disobedience
By Sölle, Dorothee
Copyright©1995 The Pilgrim Press
ISBN 13: 978-1-55635-640-7
ISBN 10: 1-55635-640-4
Publication date 9/24/2007
Previously published by The Pilgrim Press, 1995

To my children,

Martin, Michaela, and Caroline,

who are seldom obedient

Contents

Preface

THIS BOOK IS AN ATTEMPT to work through the oppressive aspects of traditions of obedience I inherited in my national, religious, and sexual identity. As a German, a Christian, and a woman, I was brought up in three traditions that demanded obedience. This fact fills me with pain, with anger, and with shame.

It is painful to discover that one obeyed the rules of a game without a clear personal understanding of where these rules would lead. One feels anger toward those who enforce obedience, and shame at being collectively obedient too long. Shame, however, is a revolutionary emotion, as Karl Marx once said: it changes those who venture to go through it.

Speaking of my own shame at being too obedient, I have to reflect on the history of my people. I have to take my national identity seriously. There is a key event that occurred in this century that stained everything before and after in German history. This event twisted words, language, ideas, and images and gave them irrevocably different meanings, stripping them of their original innocence. Take words like "star" or "hair" or "smoke," and reflect for a moment on how they could be used in 1930 and in 1943 and at the end of the century. Do they sound different? Is there a smell attached to the words when they were used after what I refer to as the "event"? Can you imagine a German writer, a person who consciously deals with language, using the word "star" as if it were nothing but a celestial lamp? Can you think of someone from my country with any capacity for remembrance who could use the word without thinking of the yellow star Jews were forced to wear before being gassed?

Again, is it possible to imagine a moral philosopher or theologian who would use the word "obedience" as if nothing had happened? It seems dangerous to me to talk about morality as a concept that is separate from history and abstracted from one's national identity. We have to own our history. Being a German after the Holocaust means that my theological concepts and the words I use to express them have no life apart from their history. Either they discuss history and try to serve grief work, or they are a meaningless religious rhetoric without remembrance and therefore without hope. I neither can nor want to forget what happened. How could I continue in the naïveté of doing theology in a suprahistorical context?

If the concept of obedience was used by idealistic or stupid young Nazis to commit the greatest crime in the history of my people, then one has to reflect on what was wrong with this concept. The results of these reflections are given in this book. A friend gave the first edition of this volume to Theodore W. Adorno in 1968. Adorno read it and was deeply impressed, as he wrote in a letter to my friend. I mention this because it highlights the connections between the Frankfurt school, which started as a critique of the authoritarian personality, and people like myself, who grew up after Auschwitz and spent so many years of their lives asking, How could it happen?

You may wonder what all of this has to say to American readers. I recall a discussion at Union Theological Seminary in New York in which a male colleague mentioned this book as being "very typically German." Another colleague, a woman, burst into laughter on hearing this remark. Obviously she did not consider obedience simply as a German matter; she knew only too well who had been victimized in America through this concept. She later told me that she recalled her mother's life when she read what I wrote here about Brecht's shameless old woman. Another student, who had listened to our conversation, mentioned Lieutenant William Calley's use of the concept of obedience to justify what he had done at My Lai. We talked about the Vietnam War and about Calley's fellow soldiers who fought and killed and died in obedience to the wrong cause. Blind obedience in which people surrender their reason and conscience to someone else is not limited to specific nations; neither is collective shame for the deeds of one's nation. There is even an international solidarity among those who feel ashamed about what their governments have done in their name, and this solidarity of shame deserves the adjective "revolutionary."

The second tradition of obedience to which this book speaks is the religious tradition, with its strong emphasis on paternal authority and children's obedience. There are three structural elements of religious obedience:

• acceptance of a superior power that controls our destiny and excludes self-determination
• subjection to the rule of this power that needs no moral legitimation in love or justice
• a deep-rooted pessimism about humans, seen as powerless and meaningless beings incapable of truth and love

Erich Fromm, in *Psychoanalysis and Religion,* distinguished between humanitarian forms of religion and authoritarian forms. The Jewish prophets, the historical Jesus, early Buddhists, and the mystics of most religions display a kind of religion that is not repressive, not based on one-sided and asymmetric dependence. This religion operates with a force that springs from the inner life of the spirit. There is one creative power in God as well as in people. Obedience presupposes duality: one who speaks and one who listens; one who knows and one who is ignorant; a ruler and those who are ruled. Religious groups that broke away from the spirit of dependency and obedience cherish different values such as mutuality and interdependence. It is precisely in the historical context of a different religion that one begins to question the social-psychological implications of the father symbol and religious emphasis on obedience. The main virtue of an authoritarian religion is obedience; self-abrogation is its center of gravity. This is in sharp contrast to a humanitarian religion, where self-realization is the chief virtue and resistance to growth is the cardinal sin.

From the standpoint of social history, such an authoritarian concept of religion affirms a given society and has a stabilizing influence on its prevailing tendencies. In this context authoritarian religion discourages any willingness to aim at greater emancipation and any critical attempt to rise above the established realities—particularly when these trends base their arguments on religious grounds: God's love and righteousness are less important than God's power. Authoritarian religion leads to that infantile clinging to consolation we can observe in the sentimentality of religious art and the history of devotionalism. But this goes together with a compulsive need for order, a fear of confusion and chaos, a desire for supervision and control.

The dangers of the religious ideology of obedience do not end when religion itself loses its spell and binding power. The Nazi ideology with its antireligious leanings proves the point that after disenchantment of the world, to use Max Weber's phrase, there is still domination and unquestioned authority and obedience. It is as though the worst qualities of religion survived its form. This is even truer today in a post-religious, technocratic culture where obedience is

seen not in terms of charismatic leaders but in terms
of the market forces of the economy, the use of ener-
gy, and the growing militarization of societies that,
without being actually engaged in war, act as if they
were. Technocrats, no doubt, have long since become
our priests. But even in the new situation where obedience is preferably spoken of in terms of "the rules of
the game," the structural elements of authoritarian
religion persist and the remaining traces of religious
education prepare the increasingly areligious masses
for an obedience from which all personal features
based on trust and sacrifice have vanished. When religion is dying out it is precisely this rigidity that sur-
vives; it is the authoritarian bonds that mostly persist
in a life understood as dominated by technocracy. The
Milgram experiment at Yale many years ago showed
that a vast majority of the ordinary people included in
the research were quite prepared, under scientific di-
rection, to torture innocent fellow humans with elec-
tric current—precisely the sort of inhumanity that
happens in a "culture" of obedience. Obedience operates in the barbaric ethos of fascism, but also in that of
technocracy.

But why do people worship a God whose supreme
quality is power, not justice; whose interest lies in subjection, not mutuality; who fears equality? Funda-
mentalism is on the rise in many places of monotheis-
tic religions. Judaism and Islam, as well as
Christianity, have developed branches of an authoritarian religion based on blind and substanceless obedience. Religious concepts such as "being saved" or

"taking Jesus as my Savior and Lord" are used without even thinking of translating them into the context of our world, as if the repetition of pious formulas could save anyone! If the concept of obedience to God is never spelled out, then it simply shores up the values of the status quo.

With the beginning of the 1990s I sense a new thrust of rigid individualism, at least in the now re-unified Europe. A peaceful development, based on socioeconomic justice and the integrity of creation, seems more distant than ever from our way of living. Authoritarian religion with its dichotomic perspective of "us" and "them" furthers the illusion of an individual salvation. It leaves out the prophetic call for justice and the understanding of our being one with God as taught and lived by the historical Jesus. It negates the humanistic and liberating tendencies in the biblical tradition and trains its followers instead for a cost-free discipleship and substance-free obedience.

There is a third oppressive tradition, apart from my national and my religious identity, that made me write this book. Coming out of German Protestantism and desperately searching for meaning inside this distorted tradition, I was not so much aware of this third power of oppression. But now I think the deepest roots to struggle with in the concept of obedience are given in my sexual identity, though I did not know this at the time the book was written. It took my American friends half a dozen years to make me aware of what I felt and wrote. When I first came to this country and started to teach at Union Theological Seminary, the faculty and students asked me again and again: What has your theology to do with your being a woman? I did not know how to respond. Of course I knew of some things I intensely disliked in male theological circles—namely, the springing from one quotation to the next in their writing without the courage to use personal discourse; the almost anal obsession with footnotes, called "scientific style"; the conscious—but much worse, the unconscious—craving for orthodoxy and the shelter it offers to the professional theologian; the neglect of historical reflection in favor of glib talk about "historicity"; the failure to evaluate and reflect on praxis.

I also felt a certain lack of candor and honesty, and I sensed no need to be personally exposed to the truth of Scripture and tradition. The theological method almost always started with "Scripture tells us . . . " After this I expected a "but" that seldom appeared. I was angry, though I did not quite understand why. When my friends exposed to me my own latent feminism I learned to understand my anger much better. In my student years I had learned to distinguish between the God of the philosophers and the God of Abraham, Isaac, and Jacob. This was a relevant and unforgettable insight. But none of these theologians then mentioned the God of Sarah, Rebecca, and Rachel. There was silence. The "fathers of the faith" were reflected in the idea of a father in heaven, but the "mothers of the faith" were left in a limbo of obscurity. They are unremembered, forgotten—in fact, repressed. This repression not only affects fifty-one percent of humankind, who as a result never found their theological voice (and maybe it wouldn't have been such an obedient voice!). It also has a catastrophic affect on the way theologians who are part of the other forty-nine percent express themselves.

Ignoring the female component of the soul and running down everything that has a feminine flavor has done more damage to the way theologians speak and write than any assault from the secular world. This purging and impoverishing process has led to the repression of the emphatic wholeness, awareness, and integration that marked the language of the Gospel. Some of the objections to the concept of obedience that are raised in this book are clearer to me now as an outcry of a woman against a so-called scientific language devoid of a sense of emotional awareness. Much of male theological language ignores the emotions of the speaking person; it is insensitive to what people experience; it has no interest and no appeal to change the world; it has no partisanship. It has a dull flatness because it leaves no room for doubt, that shadow of faith. It not only talks about obedience but also presents itself as an act of obedient talk: blind, insensitive, unimaginative, and neither reflecting nor projecting any form of Christian praxis.

A hidden feminist in me opposed this language, this virtue, and this religion. When I set out to study theology, I had no clear idea what the word GOD meant. How could anyone, given the historical situation after the Holocaust, talk about an omnipotent heavenly Being who obviously prefers to stay in the position of an observer? What was great about this God who saw and knew what happened to people in Treblinka and Buchenwald and did not intervene? Nietzsche's announcement that God is dead made a lot of sense to me, and I could describe my position as radically Christocentric. God cannot be experienced by humans. We should cling to the powerless, non-dominant Christ who has nothing more to persuade us with than his love. Christ's very powerlessness constitutes an inner-personal authority; not because he begot, created, or made us are we his, but simply because his only power is love, and this love, without any weapons, is stronger than death itself.

My difficulties with the image of God as father, begetter, ruler, and manager of history grew as I began to understand more clearly what it means to be born a woman, and therefore "incomplete," and so to have to live in a patriarchal society. How could I want power to be the dominant characteristic of my life? And how could I worship a God who was only a male?

Male power, for me, is something to do with roaring, shooting, and giving orders. I do not think this patriarchal culture has done me any more damage than it has done other women. It only became increasingly obvious to me that any identification with the aggressor, the ruler, the violator, is the worst thing that can happen to a woman.

Thus I set out to find a better theological language that could eliminate the streak of domination. I was helped by the language of the mystics.

"Source of all that is good," "life-giving wind," "water of life," and "light" are all symbols of God that do not imply power of authority and do not smack of any chauvinism. In the mystical tradition there is no room for "supreme power," domination, or the denial of one's own validity. This tradition often explicitly criticizes the lord-servant relationship and has superseded the authoritarian tradition particularly in its inventive use of language.

In the mystical tradition religion means the experience of being one with the whole, of belonging together, but never of subjection. In this perspective people do not worship God because of God's power and domination. They rather want to "drown" themselves in God's love, which is the "ground" of their existence. There is a preference for symbols like "depth," "sea," and those referring to motherhood and to nature at large. Here our relationship to God is not one of obedience but of union; it is not a matter of a distant God exacting sacrifice and self-denial, but rather a matter of agreement and consent, of being at one with what is alive. And this then becomes what religion is about. When this happens solidarity will replace obedience as the dominant virtue.

My use of the word "solidarity" tells you where I moved to from this attempt to go beyond obedience. Imagination and the claim for happiness are concepts I used in that time of transition I went through. Perhaps many people in this country may not need to hear this because the pursuit of happiness is already written into their Constitution. But there are still many others for whom the Constitution was never realized, who were told to stay in their places. Women, racial and ethnic minorities, and the poor are not freed from the culture of obedience and still must travel a long way from domination to self-determination. On this long road some of my friends who were Christians dropped religion and gave up on understanding it as a means of human liberation. I sadly disagree with them. In this sense this book is conservative and aims to convert people to "that old-time religion." During the last years we often sang this good old spiritual and we always added some new verses: "It was good enough for Sarah, it was good enough for Mary, it was good enough for Sojourner Truth, it was good enough for Mother Jones, it was good enough for Rosa Luxembourg, and it's good enough for me."

When I wrote this book I knew some things about obedience: out of the history of my country; out of the dogmatics of my religious education; and, unconsciously, out of my being a woman. What I lacked is clearer to me now, after having spent some years in the United States. I learned that there was a tradition of civil disobedience in this country. I did not know there were people who burned their draft cards with napalm and blocked trains transporting weapons to Vietnam. To hear this, to meet people who almost casually tell me they spent time in jail because of some religious and political activities, made me more aware of the alternative than before. It made me fall in love with this nonobedient tradition in the United States.

It gave me hope; it renewed my trust in the better parts of the religious tradition.

What does it mean to be a Christian in these times? Is it the tradition of obedience or the tradition of resistance we are choosing? Is there anything that goes beyond mere obedience in the Christian faith?

Beyond obedience there is resistance. I learned so much from people in the States about resistance that I would like to give something back. I hope this book can be of some help in teaching how obedience works for death and resistance for life. Imagination is needed and new forms of disobedience are required for the struggles to come. There will be a time when we will have more than the solidarity of shame.

Dorothee Sölle

Creative Disobedience

Chapter One

LEARN FROM CHRIST

WE LIVE IN AN AGE when faith in Christ is imperiled most by those who anxiously attempt to save it. They fear changes in habitual thought forms and in established ways of living. They see reform as destructive and would prefer to hide Christ in some golden shrine—untouchable and therefore incapable of relating to anyone, unchangeable and therefore incapable of transforming anyone, eternally valid and therefore removed as far as possible from our reality. But biblically speaking, God did not become human in order to remain in heaven, and changes in faith are an integral part of the history of God's divine incarnation. Incarnation means precisely that faith has a history, a history which frees our possibilities, a continuing history with an open horizon.

This open horizon is not limited to those questions which were once answered with the help of dogmatic thought forms or liturgical life styles. It is particularly open to the practical questions of Christian living. In other words, the horizon of a possible Christian ethic is also open. What will it look like? What attitudes will it foster? What individual and social virtues will be significant? What can we learn from Christ that is applicable both in our present situation and in the future?

I use the title "Christ" because it is not enough to look to the Jesus of history for instruction when one is interested in the practical rather than the historical. Precisely the person who has learned something from the life and words of Jesus finds it impossible to stop there and completely ignore the ongoing history of that same Jesus. Jesus of Nazareth has been rising for almost 2000 years! He continues to transform the consciousness of those people who believe his promises. With his coming and through his work this world's hope has grown, and thus there is increasing room for courage. In his name the face of the earth itself has been changed.

When we speak of Christ, we make what St. Francis of Assisi or Martin Luther King learned from Jesus our own. We become the possessors of treasures which human beings throughout the ages have gathered in their confrontations with Jesus. It is the Christ who has been understood, who finds concrete expression in our lives, who goes on before us, who continues to work in our midst, from whom we can learn. This is the way Christ has been taken into the present, and it has not been in vain.

But to recognize this as the way of Christ we must

keep the man from Nazareth in mind, for in history it is the misunderstood, the pared-down Christ we meet—the Christ exploited for selfish interests, the one who can be so easily manipulated. Just to use the words of our ancestors in speaking about him is to manipulate him. For by employing the language of the fathers and mothers one preserves their world and in so doing alienates the present world, whether one wants to or not. The resurrected Christ is *only* that Christ who confronts us in the present and speaks the truth about our lives today. One from whom we learn nothing, who does not transform us and sensitize our consciences, remains dead.

In no area has the ossification of traditions had more serious consequences than in the area of conscience. Under the dictatorship of established norms and behavioral patterns, the sensitivity of the conscience wilts like a plant without moisture. Even the desert cactus is unable to endure such treatment over any extended period. The concept which was responsible for this ossification in both Catholic and Protestant thought, was obedience.

For centuries the notion of what a good Christian ought to be was shaped by this single virtue. In fact it was considered the highest value of the Christian life as well as its social and religious pattern. Schiller could call on a rich, unbroken tradition when he rhymed the classic sentence: "Courage can be shown by any fool/Obedience is the Christian's jewel." Boldness and bravery were considered universal heroic virtues. The specifically Christian virtue lay in freely accepting that which was demanded, in fulfilling an assignment, in being obedient.

A theological lexicon of the 1950s speaks of obedience as the "central point and key thought of the entire Christian message."[1] Of course the meaning here is theological, that is, obedience in relationship to God. But it has its sociological and psychological consequences. What does it mean when obedience is given the central position? What are the social implications of such a theology?

Chapter Two

OBEDIENCE—
THE CHRISTIAN'S GLORY?

A BIOGRAPHICAL ACCOUNT from our own century includes the statement, "I was brought up by my parents to give due respect and honor to all adults, particularly older persons, no matter which social classes they belonged to. Wherever the need arose, I was told, it was my primary duty to be of assistance. In particular I was always directed to carry out the wishes or directives of my parents, the teacher, pastor, in fact of all adults including household servants, without hesitation, and allow nothing to deter me. What such persons said was always right. These rules of conduct have become part of my very flesh and blood." The writer of these lines, born in 1900, experienced a strict Christian upbringing, the essential content of which he presents here. At another place he emphasizes that as a child he "was brought up to obey every command without question, to be neat and orderly in all things, and to keep scrupulously clean."[1]

Under the word "obedience" in the 1927 edition of a highly respected theological lexicon appears this sentence! "Very few people are capable of achieving a wholeness of life; thus no better use of their freedom can be imagined than for them to relate to some existing whole and to associate with those above them who have achieved wholeness." Such wholeness is no longer accessible in most areas of life. Only "in the sphere of religion" does obedience have a lasting meaning, says the author (Baumgarten) who proceeds to misdirect us toward a hope, which was all too rapidly fulfilled. "So most assuredly the time will return when obedience—that is, the submission to authority, full compliance without questioning motives, the simple telling and presenting of holy things rather than the endless asking and answering of questions—will freely be acknowledged and practiced as the basis of all religious training."[2]

"Obedience to the voice of command," learned early in life, "subordination to authority," practiced until it becomes habitual, "complete submission of one's own will to the will of another which demonstrates itself in action,"[3]—in short, obedience as the cornerstone of religious education and as the key concept of the entire Christian message, is a commonly accepted Christian principle. There is no notable distinction here between Protestant and Catholic positions. The opening biographical example has its origin in German Catholicism. The author is Rudolf Höss, who was director of the Auschwitz concentration camp from May 1940 to November 1943.

What does this montage of quotations, to which one could easily add many more similar examples, have to do with a theological consideration of obedience? With what right do we bring Christian theology and social history together? What manner of comprehension, what hermeneutic lies behind such a knotting together of theological meanings, sociological realities, and political consequences? What does the obedience spoken of by those theologians, who merely repeat familiar traditions, have to do with an obedience like that of Rudolf Höss, whose father wanted him to be a priest, or Adolf Eichmann, whose parents enrolled him in the YMCA? Is it possible that Christian training in obedience can be, even partially, responsible for the good conscience of a bureaucratic murderer?

I do not mean to infer that a complex, many-faceted occurrence can be explained as being the result of a single cause. That would be an oversimplification. It is the historian's job to determine how great a part Christian training in obedience played in laying the groundwork for fascism. For the theologian it is enough to hear the repeated reference to obedience from the mouths of Eichmann, Höss, and a thousand others. One cannot help but have it stick in the throat.

Surely it is no longer possible to speak of obedience, as it is here used, with a sense of theological innocence. Nor can such innocence be reestablished by the simple assertion that of course it all has a different meaning, or by returning to the "genuine," the "proper" understanding of obedience, or by any other interpretive effort. Even the rather obvious attempt to distinguish between obedience before God and obedience before humans doesn't seem to help.

Can one demand a particular stance toward God and educate toward that stance, yet simultaneously criticize that same stance toward people and toward institutions? Is it actually possible, in the realities of daily life, to distinguish between the obedience which is due God and that obedience toward people which we can and ought with good reason refuse?

I suspect that we Christians today have the duty to criticize the entire concept of obedience, and that this criticism must be radical, simply because we do not know exactly who God is and what God, at any given moment, wills. It is no longer possible to describe our relationship to God with a formal concept that is limited to the mere performance of duties. We cannot remove ourselves from history if we wish to speak seriously about God. And in our Christian history, our history of the 20th century, obedience has played a catastrophic role. Who forgets this background or conveniently pushes it aside and once more naively attempts to begin with obedience, as if it were merely a matter of obeying the right lord, has not learned a thing from the instruction of God called history.

Chapter Three

OBEDIENCE AS SUBMISSION TO A PERSON

(An Authoritarian Model)

LET US NOW PROCEED by asking the fundamental question, what essentially is obedience? "Structurally, obedience can be defined rather accurately: it indicates a relationship in which there is an imbalance of power. At the outset fear is evidenced for the overwhelming strength of the person who asserts superiority. The anticipation of intimidation, because it has actually been experienced, soon leads to habitual obedience." Alexander Mitscherlich develops his obedience model in accordance with the experience of childhood. "The image we attach to the word obedience originates in our own earliest years, when we first learn to be obedient. We observe that one person issues commands or prohibitions, and that another obeys them."[1] Henceforth we shall refer to this model of obedience as the *authoritarian model* because it depicts obedience exclusively as a Self-Other relationship.

This Self-Other relationship can be explained in a variety of ways; Mitscherlich interprets it in terms of power and fear. These characteristics, however, may be suppressed or even replaced by others such as insight and inferiority, being informed and conformity. In no case is the relationship reversible; it can only be changed by an act of force. In this model the person who issues orders is portrayed in images such as father, ruler, owner, commander; the one who obeys as child, subject, slave, soldier.

All these images have become part of and have shaped the religious consciousness of humankind. They radiate power and at the same time convey a sense of impotency and fear. In addition to their religious functions these images also play significant educational, political, and social roles. Indeed, it can be said that there is hardly an area where religious and sociological thought forms and images have been so inseparably intertwined and interwoven as they have in the realm of obedience. God and the establishment, God and the party, God and the ordinances, God and the homeland—all demand woman's and man's obedience, and in such an indiscriminate fashion that the individual can hardly distinguish between them.

How is she to determine who or what it is that demands obedience: a power group, an imposing personality, a father figure, or ultimately, that which one tells her is God? How is she to recognize the voice of an absolute lord, when that voice does not speak to her directly, accompanied by the roar of metaphysical thunder; when, instead, she perceives it only in an indirect manner, mediated through the situations of life? Should she wait for visions or oracles—and until they occur, give her allegiance to those ruling powers who claim to be the representatives of God? How can she, having been trained in the practice of habitual obedience, keep God and all the other so-called gods apart? What standards does she need?

In any case, obedience itself is not a standard. Rather it is closer to being a kind of behavioral technique. It is striking to observe throughout the history of Christian thought how reflection on the concept of obedience has been concentrated on the practice, the technique, and the manner of obedience, to the exclusion of all objective content. Not what a person does obediently, but how rapidly, how punctually, how joyfully he obeys is important. The less one reflects on that which is demanded or forbidden, the more significant the relationship between the person who commands and the one who obeys becomes.

This is clearly demonstrated in the Rule of the Benedictine Order which holds a very prominent place in our Western world's history of obedience. Monasticism as St. Benedict encountered it generally had few regulations. The individualistic orientation of early monastics had, over the years, given way to a more communal form of life with ascetic tendencies. St. Benedict sought to regulate this communal life and its corporate activities from the viewpoint of obedience.

The position and the significance assigned to

obedience in the Rule of Benedict depart markedly from the intensely ascetic patterns of the past. For Benedict obedience is more important than living ascetically. This obedience, however, is not viewed causatively—as it was in some of the pre-Benedictine monastic traditions, where even the feeding of dogs was precisely regulated. On the contrary, St. Benedict places his entire emphasis on the relationship that exists between an abbot and the monks under his jurisdiction. This personal relationship overcomes causality. That which ought to characterize obedience is stated explicitly and repeated in a variety of ways: One should obey—without hesitation, without contradiction, without murmuring, without inner resistance, joyfully and quickly, always relinquishing all *voluntas propria.*

This new understanding has two tendencies: a reasonable moderation of strict ascetic regulations, and at the same time an internalization of asceticism as obedience. Here obedience, understood as a personal relationship to the abbot who takes Christ's place, can be viewed in two ways. A monk may obey his abbot as if he were Christ, in which case obedience becomes a means of instruction. It is a way to perfection. "Once the goal, perfection, is achieved, the student can, according to ancient monastic teaching, leave the elementary school of the cloister and enter the solitude of the desert or wilderness."

The second viewpoint, from which obedience can be considered, is far more fundamental. Here obedience is no longer seen merely as a means of instruction but achieves a value all its own. A monk obeys his abbot as Christ obeys the Father. From this point of view the abbot is not so much the faithful teacher who declares God's will, as he is the one who "as master, and in God's stead" himself carries out "the daily martyrdom of submission which the monk in obedient imitation must then also accomplish."

In this second understanding, which does not necessitate leaving the cloister after reaching perfection, we find a model of obedience in which obedience is not the way to an external goal but has itself become the goal. This model reaches complete superiority when every objective consideration of behavioral content is silenced, though this is not the case with St. Benedict. He still poses the question, "When the impossible is asked of a brother . . . ," in which case a monastic brother has the right, after accepting that which is commanded, to question it. In other words, the obedience requested is not demanded absolutely. The accent placed on the tie between monastic brothers, and the possibility of their selecting an abbot (rather than his appointment) are further developments of this nonschematic understanding of obedience.

Basically, however, in a completely authoritarian model of obedience one never asks the question "why." The world loses its significance and is degraded to being but the raw material used in practicing formal obedience. That which is done is uninteresting. When obedience concentrates itself completely on a higher and guiding "other," it becomes blind, that is, blind to the world. It hears the voice of its master in a very narrow and exclusive sense but it sees nothing. It accomplishes the act of obedience for its own sake, recognizing no additional significance.

An attempt has been made to solve this dilemma by suggesting that the obedience requested and carried out is given freely. To be sure an obedience freely given does mean a displacement of the power relationship and allows the obedient subject to maintain a certain semblance of honor. But the problem of worldlessness and the lack of objective concerns inherent in such a person-oriented obedience is only sharpened. A critique of obedience cannot satisfy itself merely by maintaining that those who obediently submit choose to do so freely. Blindness toward the world and total irresponsibility are still lacking in this variant of the authoritarian model.

An obedience that is blind to objective concerns and to the world, that merely listens to what it is told, has divested itself of all responsibility for what is commanded. Obedience and not what is to be done is the sole motivation.

Early in 1967 a United States pilot who accidentally had dropped napalm bombs on a school in which there were 27 children excused himself before the South Vietnamese government. This development led several observers to comment on the naive cynicism of the young man. Actually it is grotesque when one who has acted in obedience to a command subsequently apologizes, as if personally responsible! The very thought that this was an accident, in its naivete, bears witness to the overwhelming power of the model. The other 30,000 or 40,000 children, burned and mutilated in this war, do not matter. In blind obedience an overview of the situation and its implication is missing. In fact, the person practicing obedience dare not have such an overview. The pilot's apology itself bears witness to the absence of any real feeling of guilt. Thus obedience, when it is practiced, has the social-hygenic function of repressing guilt feelings.

In addition, a formalization of obedience that allows the content of what is demanded to become insignificant can destroy the personal relationship itself. If the contents of obedience can be exchanged so can those who issue the commands. A worldly-blind formalized conception of Christian obedience ultimately leads to volunteered obedience as an end in itself. And when it does, other authorities can easily use it for their own purposes. Once a person has been trained to be habitually obedient, the authoritarian, non-objective model functions, even under the control of other masters. When obedience is accepted as having an intrinsic value of its own, when it has become the goal of one's personal self-endeavor, the one who has subjected him or her self to it actually attains a level of masochistic self-gratification for which both the goal and the one who issues orders become insignificant.

Chapter Four

OBJECTIVITY AND OBEDIENCE

Is BLIND OBEDIENCE the only possible form of
obedience? Is it right to begin with a commanding
authority and an obedient subject, father and son,
master and servant, God and human? Is there
perhaps another model of obedience which does not
seek to understand people solely on the basis of a
Self-Other relationship? What of the more primary
dual relationship: I-Thou *and* I-It? To begin here
would necessitate the replacement of the authoritarian, and therefore subjective, model bor-
rowed from the discipline of psychoanalysis, and
allow obedience to be determined structurally as the
interrelationship of three factors: the one who demands obedience, the one who is obedient, and the
content of that obedience, its makeup.

It is essential to state clearly the nature of the dual
relationship which binds every person of whom
obedience is required. He is responsible to the one

18

who makes the demand, the person to whom he listens, and he is responsible for that which he is asked to do. In a formal sense, the real problem in obedience arises precisely when this dual relationship is overlooked and obedience is interpreted in a mono-linear sense. The entire history of obedience can be analyzed by asking whether that which is done has been reflected on or whether the guiding principle has been the rule formulated by Höss, namely that adults are "always right." Authoritarian thought and unbiased objectivity are mutually exclusive.

It appears to me that reflection on the content of a given demand, on the "what," is already called for in the Old Testament: "He has showed you, O man, what is good; and what the Lord requires of you," Micah 6:8. In this instance the "what" is said to be doing justice and loving kindness. In other words, the human being is not unconditionally placed under the demands of a sovereign ruler, whose lordship is analogous to that of an oriental despot. In the Old Testament obedience is always related to justice. Under no circumstances is it related to the ruler in a completely authoritarian manner. It always has a particular objective content.

The obedience requested of people is directly concerned with shaping the world entrusted to humans. Accordingly, the three factors of this model can be interpreted as obedience which God (the one who makes the demand) asks of humans (those who comply) for the sake of the world (the content). The object of the command is a world shaped by obedience, a human society in which justice is realized. It is not subjective spontaneity, but unbiased objectivity which alters, that is, humanizes the authoritarian Self-Other model. Every purely authoritarian form of obedience is misleading because it loses sight of the purpose for, the *telos* of, obedient behavior.

In one respect, the world view inherent in an authoritarian model of obedience is molded more by Greek than by Hebraic thought. A world ordained to continual change has little place in Greek thought, where the world is understood simply as that which is, as that which must be preserved and kept in order. Here history runs its course in natural cycles.

Where the world is understood biblically, that is, as moving toward an end, a goal, an authoritarian obedience cannot adequately express the will of God for the world. It is interested solely in the preservation of order and consequently displays hostility toward the future.

At this point it is profitable to question all the anthropological suppositions contained in the authoritarian model, to ask why the Christian-authoritarian understanding of obedience is so subjective, so monolinear. According to this view the human being is seen in her relationship to an Almighty Maker. She is that created being who is meant to correspond to the Thou of her Creator. To co-respond is to respond obediently. In fact it can be said that the human being exists "verbally," that is, in hearing and in responding. He cannot be conceived of idealistically, that is, according to some image of primeval freedom or, to speak with Sartre, according to a prototype. From the very beginning he is that being who in "primeval confrontation"[1] finds himself summoned to respond. And obedience is that form of behavior which best fits this dependent, creaturely situation.

Only in obedience does the human being accept herself as a created being, a responder, and allow the will of God, her Creator, her Addressor, to be accomplished. Christ serves as the perfect pattern for such creaturely obedience. He acknowledges that all he has is from God, he places himself completely under the judgment of God, he offers himself to God. And in this submission to power, the face of power itself is changed. It ceases to be a force or compulsion and appears in its essential nature as benevolent and life-giving grace. That which appeared to be power is accepted obediently and transformed into grace. These are the expressions Friedrich Gogarten uses to describe the destiny of Jesus, his death and resurrection.[2] Obedience is pure submission (that is, completely devoid of objective content).

The hearer is the obedient subject who, blind to the things of this world, follows only the call of an incomprehensible Creator—the divine Other. He, like Abraham, is ready to sacrifice his child or, like Kierkegaard, willing to break an engagement with Regina. The It, that is, the world of proven performance, achievement, and change, is excluded from this model. A person conceives of himself as a pure

Self to whom God lays total claim. The eternal Other demands and limits, destroys and saves humans. The exclusive nature of the divine relationship pushes all other relationships aside, and in this sense the authoritarian model of obedience can be said to be totally religious. God is here understood as a strange, wholly other power, to whom a child's lack of power most appropriately corresponds. Perhaps the religious relationship is never displayed in purer form than in the obedience of a person whose will has become identical with that of the one who summons.

But is this specifically religious anthropology, which understands obedience as the essence of a human's being, the biblical, the Christian understanding? Do we understand the divine-human relationship properly as a Self-Other relationship in this worldless and exclusive sense? Did Jesus understand it this way? Was it Jesus' purpose that we should learn obedience when he directed us to the situations of our real life? Why did he not normatively determine what God's will is instead of encouraging us to discover this will in each given situation? And finally, when Genesis 22 is abstracted from the religious-critical "interpretation" and used in the absurd radical sense of Kierkegaard, the question arises: is this God of exclusive obedience really the God of Jesus Christ?

Chapter Five

A LIBERATED SPONTANEITY

(Obedience in the Proclamation of Jesus)

THE PROCLAMATION OF JESUS provides another pattern for obedience. Here obedience is not viewed according to the authoritarian model. Its orientation is not the divine-human relationship, but the inter-relationship of three factors which, following the lead of Rudolf Bultmann, we can call "will of God," "decision," and "situation."[1] Bultmann has devised a synthesis of Kantian and authoritarian elements for his understanding of obedience. Each element is corrected by the other: Kantian blindness for the situation is corrected by the concreteness of the demand. The authoritarian blindness for the world is corrected by the necessity of making a decision (a decision which dare not be thought of as simply a reaction). Neither the traditional reflection on the how of obedience nor the direct relationship between the one who demands obedience and the one who obeys plays an immediate role.

In the proclamation of Jesus the situation in which people live, in view of which they are addressed, always comes first. Only in the situation itself can one see what obedience means now—a decision. It does not mean the carrying out of commands, and most assuredly not in the sense of Benedict's continually repeated decision to obey the abbot the way Christ obeyed God. Obedience means instead a decision which first discovers God's will in doing. The person herself must decide what is to be done; she is not the fulfiller of assigned commands. Nothing is here taken from the autonomy of the subject. The will of God does not represent external demands and it is not predetermined or fixed.

The obedient person is not the agent of fulfillment, but rather herself the legislator and lawgiver (Luther), and ever anew, because the will of God has never been formulated once and for all time. Where the divine will is thought of as fixed, that which is considered divine is of necessity misunderstood as anchored in the past—an establishment, a homeland, a right of possession. It is the situation which calls to people in a way which cannot be anticipated beforehand. It is not God in a general, timeless sense who demands obedience, but the situation which demands a response, and only therein does God require a person's response. Since the will of God cannot be determined in advance, nor the situation anticipated, the response the person makes can only be a decision in the now. He cannot find security in the Law, for the will of God cannot be discerned directly from the Law. What God wishes—and perhaps who God is—can only be determined in the situation. Such obedience distinguishes itself from good works in that life continues to remain under the judgment of the situation.

One certainly cannot say that Jesus has made it easier for people in that he requires less of them. It is something different he requires of them: an obedience which has its eyes wide open, which first discovers God's will in the situation, a discerning obedience. In an authoritarian and personalistic understanding of obedience the world is not given consideration because it is thought to be identical with a given order. In Jesus' proclamation the world takes on a concrete reality to be reckoned with. It can be ordered in a new and better way.

In an authoritarian understanding of obedience the cycle for the reproduction and transmission of obedience can be charted in the following manner:

The human being, in obedience, complies with the original order of creation by accepting responsibility for the order of the world. In this way he establishes the authority which justifies his lordship over those not yet of age. To come of age means to conform to that order and in turn assume responsibility for it.

In an objectivized and therefore liberated understanding of obedience, as Jesus proclaims it, the life cycle can be depicted as one of:

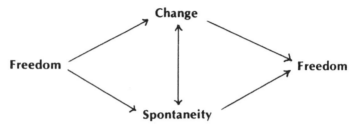

The fundamental concept of creation is that of a freedom which allows for evolutionary changes, a freedom which, since the Fall, we admittedly encounter only in a disrupted or distorted form. However, if a person is restored to freedom through the liberation of Christ, she will not merely accept responsibility for the order of the world; she will engage in transforming the world. The power she needs to change things, to discover, to invent, to set things in motion, is spontaneity. This spontaneity in turn inspires new freedom. Persons who grow up in this life cycle are not trained to find their place in a given order, but to practice freedom.

However, in the history of the church those who stressed obedience were always those for whom the world was viewed as having an autonomous, unchangeable order, an order they chose to call "created." Obedience then was always the carrying out of commands intended to maintain this order. Since the order itself was never questioned as to whether it was good and for whom, it was easy for other masters to promote obedience for different, yet comparable natural orders: that of the state, that of a master race, or that of neocolonialism, and with equal validity. The one thing these various orders have in common is their presumed reality. The obedient person remains a *re*-actor; he or she only fulfills that which is assigned; he is required to sacrifice his spontaneity on the altar of obedience.

But it is precisely spontaneity for which Jesus sets us free. That which he requires does not presuppose the order of the world; that order has yet to be established in the future. Insofar as the human must first discover what God's will is, the future of the world remains open.

In traditional usage one speaks rather descriptively of "fulfilling" obedience. The picture is that of a container of form which must be filled. So too with obedience. A previously existing order is postulated that must be maintained, defended, or fulfilled. But Jesus did not conceive of the world according to a model of completed order, which persons were merely required to maintain. The world he entered had not yet reached perfection. It was alterable, in fact, it awaited transformation. Schemes of order are in Jesus' words utterly destroyed—great and small, scholar and child, riches and poverty, knowledge of the Law and ignorance. Jesus did everything in his power to relativize these orders and set free the persons caught up in these schemes. This process of liberation is called "Gospel." Ought obedience then still be thought of as the Christian's greatest glory?

I detect that we need new words to describe the revolutionary nature of all relationships begun in Christ. At the very least it is problematic whether we can even continue to consider that which Jesus wanted under the term obedience.

Paul makes a linguistic distinction between obedience as a religious decision and obedience in the sense of submission, that is, as a form of social and political behavior. The obedience that can be equated with faith has its linguistic root in "hearing." The other word for obedience Paul uses in speaking of submission to the governing authorities is related to "ordering." This word has its source in military circles and refers to the positioning of troops in rank and file or to the ordering of battle.

This distinction between the hearing obedience of faith and a devised subordination was soon lost. And so we are left with the question whether we should accept Paul's customary usage and refer to the new stance Jesus demanded and fulfilled as "the obedience of faith," or whether another label might not be more appropriate. The overwhelming ballast of tradition ought to be sufficient warning. An accurate translation of this concept ought to contain precisely that which tradition has removed from it: objectivity and imagination. And so we must ask—is it in keeping with the truth of Jesus to attempt continually the restoration of eroded concepts by means of new interpretations?

Chapter Six

FROM THE DETERMINATION
OF OTHERS . . .

PERHAPS PHANTASY is a more meaningful and basic word for Christians in this radically changing world. What phantasy means and how it can replace the pattern of obedience is illustrated rather well by a story found in Bertolt Brecht's *Calendar Tales*.[1] Seen theologically, this story deals with "the free deed of obedience in which the new self constitutes itself in place of the old."[2] We shall let this expression of Bultmann serve as our motto.

The story is about a middle-class woman who lives her life in the prescribed manner for some 70 years. She has seven children, five of whom she raises to adulthood. She looks after the house, takes care of her husband and an assistant in his small business. She saves where she can. She cooks for a dozen people and eats the leftovers herself. She foregoes every personal pleasure. Her entire life is duty and work. When she reaches 70 her husband dies. The children have all left home, the printing business is sold without profit, and the old woman is supported by a small monthly stipend supplied by her children. But she lives out the remaining two years of her life in a way her children consider "shameless."

She stays alone in her big house without taking in the relatives who are forced to live in crowded quarters. She eats regularly in a neighborhood restaurant. She treats herself to the most improbable entertainment—movies and cards, red wine and occasional trips. She doesn't allow her visiting son to stay with her, but forces him to take a room in a hotel. She doesn't go with him to her husband's grave, and instead of taking an interest in her own family she keeps company with absolute strangers she has sought out according to an entirely new and different point of view.

The first 70 years of this woman's life are characterized by sacrificial obedience. Hers is an existence which is exhausted in working for and serving other people. This woman lives for her family. Where pleasures beckon, she foregoes them. Altruism—a life devoted to others—is demanded of her, and she offers it freely and without complaint. She meets all expectations placed on her. She is self-less (that word heard in its duality)—a person who *re*-sponds to the specific requests of others, who *re*-acts to the specific actions of others, who has developed very little individuality, very little spontaneity.

Why? Because for 70 years she never considered her own wishes and needs. Only in the last two short years of independence does a new, entirely different side of this person show itself. For so long she devoted herself to a particular way of living. Now it is as if she, the selfless one, has suddenly discovered herself in the strangely different role of an individual, with her own points of view and needs, separate from all of the common clichés.

She takes great pleasure in rising at 3 A.M. on a summer morning and walking through the empty little town. And while those who know her begin to doubt her sanity, she discovers how little she has developed as an individual during the 70 years spent in tending the family and keeping house, and how many other possibilities there have always been, possibilities for happiness, for involvement in the world, for shaping her life according to her own point of view.

It is the story of a human being who has late, but not too late, become a subject, a self-determining person. At the very end of her life, a demand once accepted without question, the demand to be there for others and to be guided by their needs, is recognized as being unrealistic and is abandoned. For too long this woman spent her life playing the roles that appeared to be assigned to her out of biological necessity. She was daughter, wife, and mother, all sexually determined roles which society is in a position to fix. Only in old age does this misused and insignificant woman achieve selfhood.

Even as one of her sons talks about being shocked by the "shameless behavior of our dear mother," in her last days she achieves a human dignity which is unthinkable without self-determination. If the theme of the first 70 years of her life has been sacrifice, obedience, and constraint, the new theme might be called spontaneity, subjectivity, or freedom.

It is easy to criticize this behavior. What, for example, becomes of the family in such a model? Isn't a certain measure of sacrifice and even self-denial necessary in every group, particularly in the family? And isn't it the special duty of a woman to keep her own desires in the background, even as her biological destiny, the bearing of children, periodically necessitates the postponement of personal desires and wishes? Doesn't nature itself in this way indicate a particular ethical position? And isn't this position of self-denial necessary for life, that is, for the continuation of biological existence, as well as for the continuation of society? What becomes of a society in which "no one wishes to serve," yet which desperately needs a sense of sacrifice, self-denial, and concern?

Bertolt Brecht did not answer these questions directly. He merely posited an antithesis to the thesis of a middle-class society. The synthesis, which ought to result from both models he depicts, is withheld because the reader of such stories is expected to discover it himself. When the text is understood, both ways of living are seen to be impossible and a third solution must be found. One avenue, however, is blocked—that which limits itself to questions of personal ethics and is interested only in the duties of the individual.

Instead, we are directed toward a society in which changes could be made to favor those on whom almost superhuman demands have thus far been made; a society in which those who have been treated as objects of demanded duty—particularly women: mothers, unmarried daughters, nurses, those of whom special dedication is expected—could become subjects capable of self-determination. Brecht, in this story, pleads on behalf of those who are exploited because of their virtues, and actually posits a society which no longer needs such virtues and which ceases to demand submission of anyone. Not only those of whom too much is demanded would profit from such a transformed society, but also all those who have anything to do with them.

A society is imagined in which it is no longer necessary to deny some people their own subjectivity. Such an inhuman demand destroys the person on whom it is made. Those who require such a degree of self-sacrifice, or include it in their life plan, lose their freedom. He who makes use of another person as a means of achieving his own ends not only humiliates that person but also degrades himself. To treat another person as if she were a thing is to become a thing oneself, a servant to the functioning of the very "thing" being manipulated. By demanding sacrifice, such a person destroys his own freedom. As the one in control he becomes the one controlled. In alienating others from that which they wish to be and can become, he alienates himself. Because he concentrates on domination, on employing others as means to his own ends, he loses all the other possibilities open to him. For example, he no longer pays attention to anything that does not fit his purpose. He loses the ability to enjoy living because he must constantly reinforce his life by accomplishments. The relationship between people is so interdependent that it is impossible for one person to prosper at the expense of another. In the long run such exploitation proves detrimental to both.

Chapter Seven

... TO THE RICHES OF SELFHOOD

WITH THIS CONSIDERATION we go one step beyond the Brecht story, but continue to focus on its content. Our hope for the establishment of a society which no longer needs the self-sacrifice of some of its members is not projected solely with the interests of those in mind who have been forced to sacrifice themselves, but also for the good of those for whom such sacrifice has all too often been made. With a closer look at the "shameless old lady," of whom Brecht speaks, and with some insight into her psychic nature, it becomes clear that the lives of those persons whom she served and for whom she offered herself could not have been very pleasant.

Habitual obedience, the apparently unqualified renunciation of one's own life, heroic behavior at the bedside of an infant or in the kitchen, these may all be indications of ethical achievement. However, the very persons whom such dedication should have benefited would have been served far better with less renunciation. Any woman who spends 70 years completely dominated by strangers and lives in opposition to her own wishes exhibits, whether she wants to or not, an existence which is permeated with restraint. The atmosphere which comes into being around persons who—even subconsciously—offer themselves sacrificially has an unavoidably stifling effect on those who take advantage of them.

The secret wishes of a person play at least as great a role in determining who she really is as does her conscious will. Dissatisfaction when it is unrecognized or suppressed spreads itself out, and the spiritual poverty of a person who constantly lives in opposition to herself is contagious. Obedience and unhappiness go hand in hand. The big house of the esteemed wife and mother was "very clean," to be sure, but we are not told if there was laughter there. And we never learn to what extent the children were harmed psychologically, or just what kind of a life the husband actually had with his self-sacrificing wife.

Transferred to abstract thought, this says: The willingness to act sacrificially is destructive and deadly when it becomes a habitual virtue, an essential function of life inherent in certain roles as that of wife and mother. The psychic masochism of the obedient person, which expresses itself as the pleasant feeling that accompanies suffering, will one day manifest itself in sadism. A person's subconscious must vindicate itself for that which is inflicted on it.

Now admittedly one can ask, and critically: What

then remains of self-dedication, altruism, and self-lessness? Is not tradition filled with a host of great and unmistakable examples of just such virtues? I believe that that which is decisive concerning the capacity for sacrificial action as a specifically human possibility can be seen most clearly at this very point. Sacrificial acts, according to our previous conclusions, can only have meaning in specific limited situations; and then they have meaning only when they are performed by persons living in harmony with themselves. All sacrifices and denials which are consistently demanded throughout a person's entire lifetime give rise to inhumanity. They perpetuate a cycle from which there is no escape: there are inhuman relationships that are maintained only by means of superhuman sacrifices, which in turn give rise to new inhuman relationships.

Selflessness is possible only where a particular level of self-awareness has been achieved. A person whose own capacity to love has been awakened, who has experienced so much happiness that it radiates from her, who has discovered her own identity; such a person is actually capable of acting sacrificially in particular situations. She can practice patience or show consideration for the ailing persons with whom she lives.

The ability to postpone one's wishes and to forego this or that is part of what it means to be human. It is not the total renunciation of one's own life which Brecht points to in his story, but the renunciation of certain concrete possibilities for personal fulfillment.

It is not a masochistic lust for punishment, but a partial renunciation freely given for the sake of another's fulfillment. A man who marries a paralyzed woman willingly gives up dancing and sport for her sake. A mother willingly gives up going out and traveling as long as her children need her. But wherever she allows this renunciation to become a habit, wherever she glorifies and perpetuates it, she actually wants her children to remain small so that she can enjoy them. In other words, she regards her children as totally dependent on her for their existence. She sees herself as an offering.

The stronger a person's self-identity—that which we have previously referred to as his or her being a subject—the easier partial renunciation becomes. In borderline situations the expression "partial renunciation" can be applied to the renunciation of one's own life for the sake of the other. However, even then it is impossible for such a person to relinquish his or her *identity* for the sake of the other. And so one could formulate the thesis: The greater one's realization of selfhood the greater one's ability for true renunciation. The more successful one is at living the easier it is for him or her to let go of life.

When a person acts sacrificially in this sense, that is, when she denies herself without casting off the identity which she is in the process of attaining, she never uses the word "sacrificial" or even the word "obedient" to describe her renunciation. These words have nothing to say about its goal, its purpose. They refer only to the act itself. Real self-sacrifice, true patience, tender concern, and all of the small attempts in which renunciation manifests itself are never understood as mere activities. When a person lets go of anything—her money, her space, her time, or even her life—she is more likely to refer to what she does as "giving." This allows her to look at the recipient, the person for whom she acts, without ever noticing her own empty hands. The ability to give grows with the riches of selfhood. It is said of the resisters in the Third Reich that they had tender and happy mothers.

Brecht's story too deals with the riches of selfhood. In her short second life the old woman befriends a deformed young girl. She, who responded to others for some 70 years of her life, now establishes a personal friendship. She, who always limited herself to doing "useful" things, goes to the movies with "that cripple," the phrase used to describe the girl by the old woman's family. She, who always scrimped and saved, purchases that cripple "a hat adorned with roses."

Chapter Eight

IN DEFENSE OF FULFILLMENT

In the last two unrestrained and therefore moral years of her life the old woman developed new and different virtues which seem more important for a developing democratic society than the older virtues. She purchased a hat "adorned with roses." At points like these in a story and in such situations of life the joyous melody of fulfillment resounds. Fulfillment? But didn't we want to talk about ethics, about virtues? About obedience and dedication, renunciation and selflessness, about the ways in which people relate to one another?

With fulfillment, on the other hand, we have certain reservations, particularly when it appears in connection with the theme of ethics. To be sure our aversion is barely formulated. It lies much deeper than we are generally aware of, and is connected with that ideology of renunciation and obedience which sees a human's self-fulfillment exclusively in opposition to his wishes and needs.

This distrust of fulfillment has found its classical formulation in antiquity, in the mythological notion that the gods are jealous of and seek to destroy those who are all too prosperous. Herodotus tells the story about the ruler of the island of Samos for whom everything resulted in personal success. His generals attain great victories for him; his fleet returns from a dangerous journey laden with goods, while the ships of stronger enemies are scattered by storms. Honor, riches, and glory are assured him. But precisely this good fortune fills his guest, the king of Egypt, with growing apprehension. With the certain feeling that things will go wrong, he pleads with his friend that of his own free will he add some misfortune, since only a considerable loss can save him from the jealousy of the gods.

Polycrates, the luckiest man in all antiquity, following his friend's wise advice, throws his most expensive ring into the sea, but to no avail. The chain of success seems unbreakable; a fisherman who has caught an exceptionally large fish hastens by to present it to the beloved ruler. In the stomach of that very fish the servants find the ring, and, not wishing to keep their precious discovery a secret, they return the ring to their master with best wishes for continued success. Hearing of this the Egyptian king breaks off his friendship in order not to be drawn into the certain demise of Polycrates.

Good fortune and fear, so it appears according to

this old tale, are indissolubly related. Success which is enjoyed thoughtlessly and without fear is punishable. Prosperity, according to the conception of antiquity is dependent on luck, indeed, it is luck. The human conceives of himself as being subject to the inscrutable powers of fate. In a later age success is depicted as the rolling ball of the Goddess Fortuna. Its path cannot be reckoned and the wise man does well never to confide in it, for it is deceitful.

To be sure success can lift one to the heights and for a limited time provide victory, honor, money, friends, and love, but there is no guarantee for the permanence of such friends. And the resigned conclusion of those who observe the ways of lives subject to luck is withdrawal to a lesser, and therefore more certain, measure of security and peacefulness. Placing excessive value on success arouses the envy of the gods.

What is the meaning of this mythical model? What social relationships does it describe? The idea that personal well-being attracts the jealousy of others, that fulfillment provokes those who are less successful, that even those who possess it often consider it unearned or even stolen, is not quite as far from our way of thinking as the ancient story might lead us to believe. Personal fulfillment can be and is enjoyed, but not apart from a comparison with those who do not participate in it. Detachment is impossible.

In a society in which all essential relationships are determined by the laws of conflict and competition, even the fortuitous well-being of an individual always appears to be possible only parasitically. And since we are accustomed to ask of everything that confronts us, What does it cost? and, Who pays for it? this question cannot be kept out of even the most private of realms; it is the contemporary formulation of polycratic fear. We experience fulfillment as something that is stolen; the more successful we are, the more like thieves we feel. From whom is this fulfillment stolen? From a workaday world, a world of production, which in itself contains few possibilities for fulfillment, and in fact has equated well-being with consumption. Yet at the same time this world is filled with hunger and exploitation from which the successful must carefully screen themselves.

Even Polycrates attempted to protect himself with the help of a sacrifice. He gave up something in order that he might retain everything. The misfortune of others is the ring which Polycrates no longer wishes to keep, the sight of which he can no longer stand, which he casts into the sea in order that he might be released from the social entanglements of his own success. The warning friend represents a consciousness of the fact that all personal well-being is socially determined; in a comparison of his position with that of others, Polycrates is terrified. But polycratic fear, a fear which is still very much alive, is not so simply disposed of. In the ring taken from the belly of the fish an awareness of the social injustice which made his own well-being possible returns to him. The jealousy of the gods is the mythical formulation of a social organization in which possibilities for fulfillment are limited and dictated by chance.

If the world is considered to be unchangeable, and if fulfillment is but a remarkable and unexpected chance occurrence within the framework of this world with its exceedingly confined possibilities for success, then striving for fulfillment must of necessity be troubled with feelings of guilt, because success is achieved only at the expense of others. The polycratic fear of the jealousy of the gods therefore finds its source in the revenge of the defrauded, those who are being cheated of their lives. As long as striving for fulfillment can be practiced only at the expense of others, and when fulfillment is seen as a private possession, then polycratic fear is inescapable. The person who only experiences the joy of fulfillment in private does not feel at one with the general public; his well-being and his happiness have no element of truth, they are not right. That is why the ring must return—and with it the certainty of ruin.

True fulfillment has to be thought of as being free from polycratic fear. She who has truly experienced selfhood need not fear that the general tendency of the world is antagonistic toward her. She knows herself as one with those around her. It is self-evident to her that the fulfillment which she herself experiences and at the same time creates, enjoys, and deals with is to be conveyed to others. Self-realization and the happiness which accompanies it are catching. So she will pose the question formulated in the Enlightenment of the 18th century concerning the extent to which the human being is "capable of creating or achieving a state of blessedness, indeed where the standard by which it can be measured lies."

He who takes up this question has already chosen sides, the side of those who assume themselves capable of achieving such a state. This is not at all self-evident. Since polycratic fear along with the ancient portrayal of fulfillment as a fortuitous occurrence was not surmounted by Christianity, self-realization has hardly ever advanced to the stage of being a theological theme. Along with the happiness associated with it, self-realization plays a minor role in the life feelings of Christian groups. In the New Testament any reference to "personal fulfillment" is excluded. Instead we find such expressions as salvation, justification, sonship, rebirth, freedom. However, this omission says nothing about the case in point and ought to give no one the right to project even the shadow of his own polycratic fear into the feelings of fulfillment and the experiences of blessedness which are recorded on its pages.

The question posed by Herder,[1] concerning people's capacity for achieving fulfillment, the self-evident "right to enjoy the earthly life" for all human beings, lies on a different level of thought, a level attested to in the Bible, but suppressed in the tradition of the church. In the Bible the world is viewed as being changeable and the possibilities for fulfillment thus provided cannot be limited by the unforeseen envy of the gods. Polycratic fear is remote from an enlightened Christian such as Herder. With the highest praise he speaks of that personal well-being which does not stand in opposition to the general tendency of history, "that open good will, that unrestricted kindness displayed by all those happy peoples of this earth who are not forced to defend themselves or seek revenge." Experiences with peoples who do not rear their children to be vengeful or defensive because they sufficiently meet their needs without the threat of punishment indicate how fulfillment is established beyond polycratic fears. That the chances for fulfillment can be multiplied means that fulfillment is not the product of luck, but is instead a matter of our freedom, a matter of our liberation. Liberated humans are builders of well-being, they are in control of all the possibilities at their disposal and not only experience but also create it.

In a comprehensive sense a person's experience of selfhood is never determined solely by that which she consumes. The delightful spontaneity of buying and selling hardly ever plays a role in the conventional understanding of fulfillment as that which is regulated by advertising. This illustrates how the capabilities for fulfillment can be destroyed, while at the same time the promises of and the opportunities for it are multiplied, differentiated, and refined.

Many of our powers are never put to work and so eventually die unused. Our ability to create something, the ability to set something in motion, the joy of making a beginning for which progress is not dependent solely on us and thus entails a risk—all these forms of fulfillment, in which the creative spontaneity of humankind achieves its own right, are threatened by that interpretation of fulfillment which sees it in acquisition, in ownership, and in consumption. Such fulfillment, though it can be purchased, is still a matter of luck. It dare not be created or produced.

Schiller has Polycrates standing on the edge of his roof waiting for what good fortune might bring. The new and more noble being, the person for whom the fullness of selfhood has become a reality, not only consumes that which falls to his or her lot, but also brings into being a new and different world. Such a sense of fulfillment will one day be named in accordance with its spiritual source. It will be called a son or daughter of God.

Chapter Nine

THE PHANTASY OF JESUS

In the interest of what we have called fulfillment, it is necessary to speak about that virtue which always flourishes among those who experience the joy of fulfillment: imagination, or better yet, phantasy. I find the best illustration of this as yet rather uncommon type of virtue in the man whose life I consider an expression of true fulfillment: Jesus of Nazareth.

To speak of the phantasy of Jesus sounds rather bold. He has always been identified with the older more traditional forms of virtue—a willingness to live sacrificially, self-denial, and obedience. But the claim which he himself made and the personal dedication which arose from that claim were far more encompassing. He worked for humanity's total reclamation, not merely for a single aspect of it.

When Jesus sharpened the Torah,[1] he radicalized the inherited commandments. Not just adultery, but the wish to commit adultery is sin; not just murder,

49

but defamation and harassment, yes, even the thought of contempt, is opposed to God's will. Now, with the arrival of God's kingdom and the inaugura-tion of a new age, more is expected of us than many theologians and pious persons ever dreamed of. No single virtue is capable of placating God. Those virtues with which people once attempted to pur-chase freedom from their awaited judgment are no longer sufficient. "Why do you call me 'Lord, Lord,'" says Jesus, "and do not do what I tell you?" Luke 6:46.

But were not those who called him "Lord, Lord" filled with piety? They had the correct confession, they kept the commandments—each one properly understood and rightly interpreted. Yet Jesus re-buked all of these evidences of their correctness, the formal confession, as well as the cultically established religious purity. What he demanded could never be accomplished by correctness. Scholars in their studies have attempted to characterize the magnitude and the severity of his claim by using expressions such as "discerning" obedience or "radical" obedience. But these additions, it seems to me, almost explode the concept of obedience because so little is left of keeping commandments. Both conscious discern-ment and radicality give rise to a spontaneity which the concept of obedience is no longer able to contain.

Jesus demands a completely awakened self-con-sciousness and a completely open acceptance of others, that is, a new way of seeing others which recognizes their fears and hopes, even when they are not clear or where they are expressed in a misunderstandable manner, yes, even where they are hidden and silent. Obedience in the sense of maintaining an established order was not sufficient for Jesus. He expected us to engage in changing the world—and it was to this end that he set free our phantasy.

Phantasy is often misunderstood, as if it were a trait which one person has and another lacks in the same way that one person is gifted musically and another is not. But that is a superficial understanding of phantasy. It sees phantasy only as some wavering form of imagination or as a dreamlike ability to escape reality. Actually, phantasy is a form of freedom which anyone can achieve during her lifetime. It comes into being like every other virtue as the result of our encounter with the world. It arises out of the education we have received and from the experiences we have had.

A person can, during the course of his lifetime, become more imaginative, or, on the other hand, he can give up more and more of his phantasy. He then becomes progressively poorer in his style of living and ever more fixed in that which he refers to as his life-experience or his understanding of people. This growing impoverishment of life takes pleasure in assuming the appearance of maturity, in feigning a full awareness of reality. However, it is in fact a surrender of the sense for possibilities, of that phantasy which bursts all boundaries. As a person limits herself to that which she finds, which she preserves and sets in order, her spontaneity atrophies. She ceases being a child—so people say—without realizing the loss expressed in this manner of speaking. Ceasing to be a child she loses the world of dreams, of poetry, of play, and thus the world of possibilities.

This limited awareness of reality plays a remarkable as well as a fatal role in the attitudes which many took toward Jesus. Fishermen are fishermen and belong at their nets—he who disturbs this order and makes wandering preachers out of uneducated fishermen is unrealistic. Illnesses, particularly those of a chronic nature where there is no acute danger to life, can be dealt with during the week. He who is concerned about other persons on the Sabbath, instead of keeping the religious commandments concerning God and the holiday rest, bursts established boundaries. He who tolerates or even favors foreigners and people of a different faith has removed the boundaries of the national religious consciousness—his soaring phantasy really acknowledges but a single principle: the creation and the propagation of well-being.

Jesus made people whole without asking for thanks. He fulfilled people's wishes without questioning their validity. He allowed phantasy full reign, without bowing to propriety. He took seriously the religious requirements such as fasting, the breaking of bread, and thanksgiving, but he was also able to put them all aside. He was at ease with friend and foe alike. The conventional classification of people into artificial groupings could be suspended at any time.

He never brought new virtues and duties. It was

fulfillment he offered to those with whom he dealt, a certain sense of wholeness, of well-being, which made virtue and its practice possible. He did not fulfill duties; instead he changed the situations of those whom he met. His phantasy began with the situations but always went far beyond them.

Perhaps his boundary-breaking phantasy can be most clearly seen in the framework of the vocation which he chose and which of course included a traditional vocational ethic. Jesus became a rabbi, a teacher, but he never allowed himself to be tied down to the rules of the teaching game. For the Pharisees the one decisive rule of that game was the authority of their heritage. They established the truth of each sentence on the basis of Scripture. Because it was written down, because it had been of help to the fathers, therefore it was true, therefore it must have come from God. No Pharisee would ever have dared to speak like Jesus who placed his personal authority above that of Moses. "You have heard that it was said in times past . . ." Matthew 5:21. Thus Jesus began his well-known antitheses in the Sermon on the Mount, but not in order to continue, "So now it is up to you also to keep the Law and the Prophets and do what you are told." Jesus surpassed these old precepts which stood under the highest authority of Moses when he said, "But I say unto you. . . ."

CHAPTER TEN

A PERSON SAYS "I"

JESUS WAS A HUMAN BEING who risked saying "I" without support or backing. It was not because he held an official position, had influential friends, or possessed excellent recommendations that he spoke this way. Ever since the close of his earthly life his friends as well as his foes have attempted to provide a backing for him which would allow them to disregard the unbelievable phantasy of his love. But Jesus' freedom, his "but I say unto you," remains unavoidable. His friends asked for miracles that would substantiate his authority, but it was precisely such miracles he refused to perform. His enemies awaited equally tangible proofs of divine approval. While he was still on the cross they cried out to him, "Come down from the cross, and we will believe." But Jesus did not come down. Nor did he turn stones into bread in the wilderness, or spring from the pinnacle of the Temple, or become a performer of medical miracles, or, as the apocryphal gospels relate, clap his hands and have 12 sparrows drop dead at his side.

All of this would have represented a step backward, a little less freedom, a bit more authority for him, and at the same time a little less liberation for others. All of this would have strengthened that consciousness of reality which is oriented toward material existence. All of this would undoubtedly have led people to accept Jesus, but it would not have changed the world in which they themselves lived; it would only have reproduced that world. To be sure these evidences of power and this approval of God could have spared Jesus from death (after all, God still has the strongest legions); but they would not have helped people to achieve selfhood, to be free— or in the language of mythology—to rise with Christ.

When Jesus said "I" in this unique sense, without backing—"I" forgive you your sins, "I" say unto you arise, "I" call you, come—he thereby transformed the reality of the people in whose company he stood. We find ourselves within a limited and given framework, within a constellation of fixed factors. Sensitive people, such as poets, even speak of the prisons into which we have been placed, and in their portrayals suggest that this condition of limitation and fixation only appears to be natural, that in reality it has definite social causes which are alterable. When Jesus in the manner in which we have described said "I," he lifted the so-called natural limitations of human life. His phantasy accepted no limits. In the power of his world-transforming phantasy he set aside the boundaries of nations, of social classes, of education, of sexual distinctions, of religions. Indeed, whatever it might mean in the language of myth, he conquered that boundary which more than any other imprisons us, the boundary between life and death.

What power made these conquests possible? How can we adequately picture what took place? What enables a person to say "I" as Jesus did, to fill the role of "God" for others, to be free from the fear of death and concern about the afterlife, free from inhibitions and cautions, free from demands on one's self and the longing to be recognized and accepted, free, completely free for other people—from where does one take such freedom?

Of all humans who ever lived I consider Jesus of Nazareth the person most conscious of his own identity. And I am of the opinion that the strength of his phantasy must be understood as rising out of this joyous self-realization. Phantasy has always been in love with fulfillment. It conceives of some new possibility and repeatedly bursts the boundaries which limit people, setting free those who have submitted themselves to these boundaries which thereby have been endlessly maintained. In the portrayal of the Gospels Jesus appears as a man who infected his surroundings with happiness and hope, who passed on his power, who gave away everything that was his.

The conventional picture of Jesus has always placed his obedience and his self-denial in the fore-

ground. But that phantasy which is born of fulfillment is a far better description of his life. Even his
death could not be fully understood; indeed, it would
be misinterpreted as the tragic end of one who had
been a failure, if the possibility of the resurrection
had not already been present in him. But the
resurrection as the ongoing truth of Jesus' cause was
present in his death. He never retracted the statement "I am the life" even in death.

Should one consider the death of Jesus from the
point of view of obedience alone, one would overlook
the fact that selflessness and a readiness to live
sacrificially are possible only when a person has come
to himself and has reached the fullest level of
personal freedom. Obedience only makes sense when
it is expressed by a person who is in harmony with
himself. All self-sacrifice, all self-denial, and all suffering which is expressed without this harmony, that
is, simply because it has been demanded by others, is
senseless and produces nothing. It cannot issue in a
resurrection.

The selflessness which rests on the experience of
self-realization is something quite different. Here the
potential for love is already awakened, and the air of
well-being which a person can radiate provides the
clues which lead directly to that which she has
experienced. The person who thus lives out of the
riches of her own fulfilled self can give up a number
of her own wishes, she can postpone them in view of
the wishes of others, she can store up wishes and
project them to different objects. She has become

flexible in her wishes and does not have to fix them solidly on definite goals in the way that the obedient person, for example, must confine herself to carrying out assigned duties.

The liberated human being is so strongly aware of him or herself as a self-determining subject that partial denials become possible. The expression "partial denial" may seen inappropriate when it is applied to Jesus, but I use it in order to underscore the fact that a person can never deny his own identity simply at the will of another. In this sense Jesus too never denied his own identity. It is more appropriate to say that his death was the final substantiation of his identity, of the unheard of assertion "I am the life."

Expressed in more traditional, older religious language, that would mean: A person can indeed give up his own existence for the sake of others, but one can never sacrifice that life which is eternal. Even when one is of the opinion that he has actually sacrificed his own eternal life, his "soul," the devil is the true recipient. That soon shows itself in the results of such a diligent and sacrificial obedience— the realm of exhausting performance and inner dissatisfaction encroaches on everything. The same holds true for Jesus despite every heteronomous attempt to substantiate his way of life. The greater the self-realization, the greater the capacity for self-sacrifice.

And it is this that we can learn from Christ. The more fully one is aware of one's own identity, the easier it is for him to let go of himself. His hands do not grasp vice-like that portion of existence which has come his way. Since he has experienced and can call the fullness of life eternal his own, he is not out to hold fast. He can open his hands.

Chapter Eleven

THE FULFILLMENT OF CHRIST

B ECAUSE ALL THINGS are Christ's, heaven, eternal blessedness, the kingdom which he proclaims and establishes, he need not hold them fast. The life, which he himself is, is not separated and isolated from that larger life he refers to as God. He feels himself so permeated and supported by that greater life, so completely accepted and loved, that for him fulfillment is not something to be produced or acquired. For him fulfillment is always a given, that which authenticates his Gospel. It enables him to say "I" and it frees his phantasy for others.

Fulfillment liberates the self from its established boundaries. Fulfillment destroys the prisons which limit the self and channel its energies. Once freed, they thrust themselves into the adventure of new life—in the phantasy which produces freedom and devises opportunities for others to experience true selfhood. There is an essential relationship between the self, its fulfillment and its phantasy, a relationship which becomes evident in the life of Jesus but is equally valid for all people.

When one attempts to describe this relationship in terms of traditional theology, one must speak of grace, of the justification of the sinner, and of the sanctification of the world. In that grace which appears in such a way that a person's life is fulfilled, a new self, an "I," comes into being which is removed from the realm of one's own fears, which is freed or redeemed. And precisely this new self can no longer see its task as carrying out given rules or regulations, can no longer establish a Christian ethic on the basis of obedience since the task now is to transform the world, a task which requires the virtue of phantasy.

In the history of philosophy there is an age-old debate between those who begin with the joy of fulfillment and those who begin with virtues and duties. This debate has never been concluded as ought to be the case in all philosophical problems. It is only in the practical action which is possible in a self-determining society that the answer can be found. At least it is possible to imagine a society in which the answer to this question is not predetermined by a few for the many, but rather in which the individual him or herself can determine the ways in which he or she will practice virtue. The results would show *how* problematic and destructive it is to demand obedience of a specific group of people when the obedience which is demanded has been made necessary by a previously fixed set of social constellations.

The system in which such thinking occurs dictates

obedience for children, abstinence for youth, and selflessness for women, and demands that men struggle for accomplishment. A human being must be able to determine what form the expression of his virtue should take in the light of the particular situation in which he finds himself; he must be able to influence every situation, and he must be able to participate in determining all of them. Spontaneity, participation in determination, and freedom are the conditions for every virtue that has risen above the level of the animal kingdom, above the realm of necessity and training.

The psychic base for the newer virtues then is no longer obedience which is measured according to norms, which accepts the difficulties of a situation, which supports order and willingly endures that which must be endured. The new base is phantasy. In fact it may be said that phantasy is the mother of all of tomorrow's virtues. For centuries things happened in the family of virtues much like they happened in the best of marriages which our outdated social system was able to produce; in order for life to be bearable, wives were forced to deceive their husbands time and time again. In a similar way phantasy had to deceive its parent, obedience, over and over again in order to establish even the most fleeting of human relationships.

Today, since obedience no longer claims the authority of a father figure, phantasy and all of its children are once more free to establish a better kingdom. Their energies are no longer expended in evolving new methods of deceit. Having been liberated, they begin each new day with the adventure of virtue: the discovery of ever new and different experiences of fulfillment. Phantasy loves fulfillment; it cannot help but be creative. It destroys the mechanics of force which controls those people who deny themselves as well as those who must accept this self-denial. It infects its surroundings with a new zest for life.

It is possible to conceive of an ethical system in which all virtues that do not need our phantasy become superfluous. Obedience would be replaced. Order, punctuality, cleanliness, economy, and diligence—to name but a few of the virtues of obedience—would only make sense where they serve the purpose of establishing empathy with one's fellow human beings. Punctuality has no value in itself, but phantasy knows how, in certain situations, the lack of punctuality can prove harmful. Disorderliness is no failure, but it can slow our powers of concentration and attentiveness. It can rob us of time; indeed, it can dim the joy that a fulfilled person radiates.

It is possible to conceive of an ethical system in which all virtues find their source in phantasy. A few such virtues, which have already become exceedingly important for the private life of persons living closely together, are tolerance and humor, righteous anger and empathy, initiative and the cultivation of a productive power of imagination.

The phantasy of Christ is a phantasy of hope, which never gives up anything or anyone and allows concrete reversals to provoke nothing but new discoveries. The phantasy of faith holds fast the picture of a just society and never allows itself to be talked out of the kingdom of righteousness. Phantasy is the "gewusst wie," the "know how" of love. It never retires before it has achieved some new insights. It is inexhaustible in the discovery of new and better ways. It is ceaselessly at work improving the welfare of others. This form of transcendence was all but lost by Christians shortly after Jesus of Nazareth walked this earth; to them otherworldly transcendence seemed more appropriate.

The creative spontaneity of the human freed by fulfillment disappeared from consciousness. Only traces of its presence can be detected throughout the history of the church. As payment for the damages incurred a second world was projected, a replica intended to take the place of this one. "God" no longer was, as had been in the life of Jesus, the one who made it possible for a person to say "I." Rather God was, and today still is, used for the creation and sustenance of a higher or "superior-self," which establishes the kingdom of obedience and its derived secondary virtues—order, economy, punctuality, cleanliness, and diligence over those impulses and drives which must of necessity be subdued.

It appeared to be forgotten that for Jesus "God" meant liberation, the unchaining of all powers which lie imprisoned in each of us, powers with which we too can perform miracles which are no less significant than those we are told Jesus himself performed. The feeling of possessing a full life, the fulfillment of Jesus, was lost. It was as if one wished to promise people something more and greater than the fulfillment of Jesus—a participation in divine life which is realized only after death. With the help of this beyond, this still to come, fulfillment was defamed, and the transformation of this earth in view of the possibilities for fulfillment remained subordinate.

We still secretly feared that the realization of selfhood could only be achieved at the cost of others, suspected that it was the robbery of others, because we viewed the earth itself and the projected possibilities for fulfillment as constant and immovable. If instead the world is seen as moving toward a goal, if God is experienced as active in history and not merely posited as resting beyond nature, as eternally being, then the possibilities for fulfillment are multiplied. Then phantasy ceases to be a thing for children and poets—that which Christian history has made of it. The person is once again given the courage to say "I," without, in so doing, taking anything from anyone else. On the contrary, the "Mensch" who has experienced selfhood, the person able to say "I," can have an entirely different and liberating effect on all who have anything to do with him. The person whose relationship to others is directed solely from some "superior-self" cannot possibly have such an effect on others.

Perhaps one can say that all the great saints throughout the history of the church lit the lamp of phantasy anew. But it is just as certain that all of the great churches maintained themselves on the basis of obedience and were more appreciative of obedient Christians than of those who realized the phantasy of Christ in their own lives. This phantasy has nothing to do with filling out already existing structures. Its whole aim is rather to discover, make visible, and disclose that which is invisible. God, according to Christian tradition, so came into our lives as to become discoverable—God can be recognized in the face of the person who lives next door. God can be found in those fixed orders which we can alter despite their apparent ossification. God, the eternally active Creator, becomes visible in our world of time and space.

Appendix

FROM MYTH TO IDEOLOGY

(An excursus concerning the methodology of criticism)

OUR PROBLEM TODAY is not so much myth as it is Christian ideology. Just to open the Bible and expect to receive instruction is not sufficient, not even when the methods of textual criticism and demythology are employed. The person who seeks to determine the nature of obedience according to its original New Testament meaning cannot be absolved from the recognition that its original nature is imbedded solidly in history. An existential-theological hermeneutic of meaning oversimplifies the issue by springing directly back and forth between the first and the 20th centuries. Such an impressive leap is capable of moving the heart of an individual; but the social reality, which has in part been formed by the educational practices of the Christian church, remains untouched.

67

Can theology afford to ignore the social history of Christianity? Can hermeneutics afford to proceed only from the word of Scripture in an effort to confront us with this abstract word apart from its accomplishments, devoid of its own history? In so doing, the very Reformation heritage which is supposedly preserved is actually denied. For Scripture to become the "Word of God," that is an enlightening, active, world-transforming event, there must be a reflection on and an understanding of one's own situation. A hermeneutic of meaning remains unhistorical, despite and directly because of the historical-critical method, so long as it does not include a hermeneutic of results and consider theologically actual historical accomplishments. It is not enough to ask what obedience is "essentially"; we must know what the results of such obedience are in order to recognize what it is capable of becoming.

For this reason it can be said that demythology misunderstands itself when it concentrates only on the texts of the New Testament and becomes a definitive process. To be of real value it must delve into the continuing history of transmission and examine the basic elements which necessitated such a transmission. A demythology of this kind will of necessity lead to ideological critique.

Today, in reflecting on our faith, we seldom deal with the world of mythology. This comparatively colorful and beautiful though non-obligatory world has all but ceased to exist. Nevertheless its derivative, a distilled and rationalized ideology, has become extremely troublesome. Myths can die when they no longer give expression to the actual life relationships of people, their needs, their worries, their fears, their hopes and wishes.

A mythical story about a miraculous healing no longer means anything to all those persons who have learned to place their hope in penicillin. In a mythological worldview such concepts as "sickness" and "heaven" have an entirely different meaning than they do in a critical-rational understanding of the world. However, if a myth which has expired is maintained in its traditional form, it hardens into an ideology, into an overarching principle which is no longer related to the practice of real life. In this case the word "ideology" is understood as a consciousness in which the theory and practice of a group of people have nothing to do with one another nor do they correct one another.

The overarching principle is neither touched nor changed by that which actually occurs in life. There are theologians who are so ideologically isolated that a happening like Auschwitz never moves them to alter their position. Since such an overarching principle does not take practical life into account, it has no possibility of affecting or altering the course of practical life. Rigor mortis is complete.

In mythical thought where God appeared directly in summons and command, in natural phenomena and changes of fortune, a concept like obedience had a different meaning than it does in the modern view of human self-determination. That which had its rightful place in mythology becomes an ideological relic in our post-mythical age. Such a relic tends to cloak the interests of those who care for and pass on dead myths. The assertion that "the essence of faith is obedience" is as formal as it is empty, and requires ideological critique rather than interpretation.

It makes no sense to demythologize the New Testament and then to present it in its purified form to a society caught up on post Christian ideologies. The weakness of many exegetically sound and theologically correct sermons has its source here. Instead, the practice of demythology, developed in New Testament studies, must find its practical place as an ideological critique in the contemporary social scene.

The present level of scientific specialization in our world makes it impossible for any single discipline to accomplish this; it will take a cooperative effort. There is nothing more catastrophic for a hermeneutic of meaning, especially for one which understands itself as the "language instructor" of faith, than to be isolated from other human disciplines. Yet this situation is typical in the broader circles of existential theology and is fed by a traditional prejudice against all non-theological disciplines, especially those most modern such as sociology, political science, psychology, and psychoanalysis. This theological arrogance toward that which is "merely" psychological or sociological goes hand in hand with a form of ignorance which believes that it is possible to develop an ethic solely on the basis of the past.

A demythology which does not become an ideological critique reinforces the ideological veil that hangs above our social reality simply because its partial explanations create an elite sense of complete enlightenment. Yet obedience needs an ideological critique and not merely an exegetical definition.

Notes

CHAPTER 1

1. See article on *Gehorsam* (obedience) by F.K. Schumann in *Die Religion in Geschichte und Gegenwart,* 3rd edition (Tübingen: J. C. B. Mohr, 1955).

CHAPTER 2

1. Rudolf Höss, *Kommandant in Auschwitz: Autobiographische Aufzeichnungen* (Munich: Deutscher Taschenbuch Verlag, 1963), pp. 25 and 46.

2. See article by Baumgarten on *Gehorsam* in the 2nd edition of *Die Religion in Geschichte und Gegenwart* (Tübingen: J. C. B. Mohr, 1927).

3. See article on *Gehorsam* in *Stuttgarter Biblisches Nachschlagewerk,* 1950.

CHAPTER 3

1. A. Mitscherlich, *Auf dem Weg zur vaterlosen Gesellschaft* (Munich: 1963).

CHAPTER 4

1. See *Gehorsam, RGG,* 3rd edition.

2. F. Gogarten, *Jesus Christus Wende der Welt: Grundfragen zur Christologie* (Tübingen: J. C. B. Mohr, 1966), pp. 53ff.

CHAPTER 5

1. R. Bultmann, *Jesus and the Word,* (New York: Charles Scribner's Sons, 1958), translated by Louise Pettibone Smith and Erminie Huntress Lantero, pp. 52ff.

CHAPTER 6

1. B. Brecht, "Die unwürdige Greisin," in *Kalendergeschichten,* Vol. 77 (1953) p. 114.

2. R. Bultmann, *Theology of the New Testament* (New York: Charles Scribner's Sons, 1951), translated by Kendrick Grobel, Vol. 1, p. 316.

CHAPTER 8

1. J. G. Herder, *Ideen zur Philosophie der Geschichte der Menscheit,* Vol. 8, iv and v.

CHAPTER 9

1. H. Braun, *Gesammelte Studien zum Neuen Testament und seiner Umwelt,* (Tübingen: J. C. B. Mohr, 1962), pp. 75ff.